Pr

"As an observer of psych[...]elieve that Mercedes's channeling [...]wed in the trance state by real beings who can [...] ary Magdalene. When I listened to this channeling I was blown away."
—Dr. Lorenzo da Costa, MD

"A most profound revelation of what the Holy Grail is—shining a light on the complementary roles of Magdalene love and Christ consciousness."
—Robert "Han" Bishop, PhD, host, "Transforming Reality Talk Show"

"A book filled with uplifting insights for these modern times. Read it and read it again, for each chapter contains a gem of wisdom and inspiration."
—Ton Van der Kroon, men's work pioneer and author, *The Return of the King*

"These messages are the key to finding true happiness and wholeness in today's world."
—Amara Karuna, Sufi minister and spiritual counselor

"*The Holy Grail* is a roadmap to humanity's higher octaves, where our collective Sacred Masculine will indeed unite with the Divine Feminine."
—Sheil Seclearr, filmmaker, "The Water Clock"

"I want every human on the planet to read this book."
—David Spinney, New Consciousness workshop facilitator

"These profound messages bring new information about the Divine Feminine and Masculine. I think it's important that this is brought to the world at this time."
—Jacqueline de Rond, clinical psychologist, "Awakening the Illuminated Heart" workshop leader

"This is an amazing book! *The Holy Grail* brings the Sacred Masculine and Divine Feminine together in a way that will truly mesmerize the serious reader. Be prepared to learn and grow spiritually."

—**Ronald Tobin, spiritual counselor and hypnotherapist**

"The revelation of the true meaning of the Holy Grail is far richer and more beautiful than any of the mythical and mystical explanations presented hitherto, warming my heart and touching the deeper recesses of my soul. I highly recommend this book."

—**Anant Akash, PhD, psychologist**

"This seminal work offers many secrets about the nature of reality, Christ Consciousness, and beyond. These teachings from Yeshua and Mary Magdalene help us to understand more about ourselves, each other, and the divine so we may walk in their footsteps—fully human and fully divine."

—**Dr. Melissa Sophia Joy, ND,
founder, Sophia Healing Academy and Somatic Awakening**

"As a man who's been doing spiritual work and men's work for nearly forty years (and by the way, a channeling skeptic), I say without hesitation that every man should read this book. What you will find here is an understanding of the seeming conflict between the Masculine and Feminine, how to honor the polarity that is who and what we are divinely ordained to embody, and how that polarity is destined to fuel our ascension to our true source. This book is an opportunity not to be wasted."

—**Stan Eads, King-Warrior-Lover-Magician**

"This book will impact people in a big way—helping to see what's possible in sacred union."

—**Richard Alexander Arsic, men's work facilitator**

"Mercedes is a clear conduit for both Yeshua and Mary Magdalene. I highly recommend this book for all spiritual seekers."

—**Stanley Sabre, poet and spiritual warrior**

The Holy Grail

Sacred Masculine

Divine Feminine

The
MAGDALENE–YESHUA
Teachings

MERCEDES KIRKEL

Published by
INTO THE HEART CREATIONS
Rio Rancho, New Mexico
www.mercedeskirkel.com

Copyright © 2023 by Mercedes Kirkel

All rights reserved. No part of this book may be used or reproduced in any manner whatsoever without written permission, except in the case of brief quotations embedded in critical articles and reviews.

Paperback ISBN: 9798987663301
Ebook ISBN: 9798987663318

First edition

Names:	Kirkel, Mercedes, author.
Title:	The Holy Grail : sacred masculine & divine feminine / Mercedes Kirkel.
Description:	First edition.	Rio Rancho, New Mexico : Into the Heart Creations, [2023]	Series: The Magdalene-Yeshua teachings.
Identifiers:	ISBN: 979-8-9876633-0-1 (paperback)	979-8-9876633-1-8 (ePub)	LCCN: 2023901365
Subjects:	LCSH: Mary Magdalene, Saint (Spirit)	Jesus Christ—Spiritualistic interpretations.	Grail—Psychological aspects.	Self-actualization (Psychology)	Channeling (Spiritualism)	Guides (Spiritualism)	Inspiration.	Civilization, Ancient—Controversial literature.	Feminist theology.	Femininity of God.	Masculinity—Religious aspects.	Masculinity of God.	Gnosticism.	Mysticism.	Spiritual life.	Spirituality.	Mind and body.	Spirit writings.	BISAC: BODY, MIND & SPIRIT / Channeling & Mediumship.	BODY, MIND & SPIRIT / Angels & Spirit Guides.	BODY, MIND & SPIRIT / Inspiration & Personal Growth.	BODY, MIND & SPIRIT / Ancient Mysteries & Controversial Knowledge.	BODY, MIND & SPIRIT / Mysticism.	BODY, MIND & SPIRIT / New Thought.	BODY, MIND & SPIRIT / Spiritualism.	SOCIAL SCIENCE / Men's Studies.	SOCIAL SCIENCE / Women's Studies.
Classification:	LCC: BF1290 .K572 2023	DDC: 133.93--dc23

Cover art by Vaclav Vaca
Book design by Michelle M. White

To Yeshua and Mary Magdalene,

*For opening the secrets of the universe,
as well as our hearts.*

Contents

Preface ix

Note to Reader xi

PART I ~ THE QUEST OF HUMANITY

1. The Holy Grail Message 3

PART II ~ HIGHER MASCULINE AND FEMININE

2. Christ Consciousness 19
3. Magdalene Love 25
4. God as Masculine *and* Feminine 31
5. Exalted Masculine 33
6. Exalted Feminine 37
7. Embracing the Feminine as Beloved 39
8. Yeshua and Mary Magdalene as Models 41
9. Yeshua and Mary Magdalene as Complements 43

PART III ~ THE JOURNEY

10. Your Higher Self 47
11. Unconditional and Conditional Love 49
12. Seeing the Higher Masculine and Feminine 53

PART IV ~ SACRED MASCULINE IN LIFE

13. Sacred Warrior 57
14. Sacred Magician 61
15. Sacred Lover 63
16. Sacred King 67

PART V ~ DIVINE FEMININE IN LIFE

17. Feminine-Masculine Differences 71
18. The Feminine is Cyclic 75

PART VI ~ UNION

19. The Circle, the Cross, and the Arrow 79

PART VII ~ THE CALL

20. The Prayer of Heart-Light 83

Notes 85

About the Author 89

Books and Videos by Mercedes Kirkel 91

Preface

I'M A SPIRITUAL CHANNEL, which means I communicate with higher beings. I've been blessed to communicate with many amazing beings, but especially with Mary Magdalene and Yeshua (Jesus).

My channeling began in 2010 when Mary Magdalene first came to me. Over the course of a month, Mary downloaded an entire book of groundbreaking spiritual wisdom to me. Those messages are recorded in *Mary Magdalene Beckons*.

After the publication of that book, I spent a number of years helping people understand and apply Mary's teaching in their lives. Throughout that time, I witnessed over and over again how transformative Mary's process is, especially for women. But few men seemed interested in Mary's instruction, and the few who were often had a harder time understanding and implementing Mary's teaching than the women I worked with. I'd always assumed Mary's guidance was equally important for men and women, since her focus on heart-based living felt universal to me. But I started to wonder if my assumption was correct.

At a certain point, I asked Mary Magdalene, "Is there a different spiritual path for men?" To my great surprise, she replied, "Yes."

"What is it?" I asked. This book contains the response I received from Mary Magdalene and Yeshua.

The messages they proceeded to give filled me with awe and excitement. This was information that I hadn't heard elsewhere—beginning with their explanation of what the Holy Grail really is. And they continued with so much more, addressing fundamental human questions vital to men and women: Why are we here on Earth? What's our purpose? Where is humanity headed? Are there differences between men and women (beyond the obvious physical ones)? What's the path for me?

Yeshua and Mary more than answered my initial question about the spiritual path for men. They gave me a trove of new information centered on the cosmic roles of the Sacred Masculine and the Divine Feminine. This wisdom is extremely timely and greatly needed because there's so much confusion in our world regarding the Masculine and Feminine. Yeshua and Mary's universal—yet very practical—guidance empowers us as men and women, Masculine and Feminine, evolving together on our evolutionary quest.

As valuable as their teaching is, there's another gift that Yeshua and Mary bring in these pages that I cherish even more: their profound love. Yeshua and Mary love the Masculine and Feminine, and they model that love through their instruction, as well as their relationship with each other. That love is available to all who read their words. It's a taste of sacred love that feeds the heart and nourishes the soul.

Welcome to the Holy Grail. May this potent knowledge guide your course into the future. May it guide us all.

Note to Reader:

The terms "Feminine" and "Masculine" used throughout this book refer to the archetypal Feminine and Masculine that reside within all of us (regardless of our gender) and within all of manifestation. The twin concepts are similar to the concepts of yin and yang in Eastern philosophy.

PART I

THE QUEST OF HUMANITY

ONE

THE HOLY GRAIL MESSAGE

Yeshua: Hello, dear ones. This is Yeshua.[1] I am moved to speak to you about the Holy Grail because understanding the Holy Grail is extremely important for humanity at this time.

Humanity is at an important juncture. I might say it's a "critical" juncture, but not in the sense of bringing criticism or of being dire. Rather, it's a very significant juncture. In some ways you could say that all of human history on Earth up until now has led you to this point. And you (meaning humanity) are showing the signs of readiness and actualization of moving into this tremendous change. There are many ways this change could be described and viewed, but the Holy Grail is a good way of approaching it because so many people relate to the idea of the Holy Grail.

I am going to begin with some of the interpretations and understandings of the Holy Grail that have been put forth in the past. I then want to explain how that is different from what I would like to share with you and how I suggest the Holy Grail can be viewed. So, let us begin by looking to the past.

The Holy Grail has been said to be associated with me. Some say it is the cup or chalice that I drank out of at the last supper (as recorded in the Bible).[2] Some say that chalice was used by Joseph of Arimathea[3] to capture my blood at the crucifixion.[4] There are claims that this chalice was transported to England or Scotland, perhaps by Joseph of Arimathea, and is now connected with particular churches there (including declarations of being buried in the ground at those sites). Some say the chalice is connected to or located at other sites.

There are also associations with the Holy Grail later in history. Some believe the Holy Grail was part of what the Templars[5] were seeking to find—or perhaps found—in their journeys to Jerusalem and the Holy Land.[6] This was approximately one thousand years after my incarnation. Some say the persecution of the Templars that occurred at the beginning of the Inquisition[7] was associated with the Templars having the Holy Grail.

The Holy Grail has also been associated with King Arthur and the Knights of the Round Table.[8] It's been suggested that the knights were on a quest to recover the Holy Grail, and some assert that one or more of the knights found it.

More recently it has been proposed that the Holy Grail was not a cup or a chalice that I drank out of but rather, it was Mary Magdalene.[9] Those who suggest this say that Mary was the vessel of my love, or the receptacle of our love together through our lovemaking and through bearing our children, all of which made *her* the Holy Grail.

Some have put forth that the Holy Grail is about Mary Magdalene (or perhaps Mary and me both) going to France after the crucifixion. They maintain that through having children, we began a bloodline that carried our lineage. This lineage was given the French name of *Sangreal*,[10] which can be interpreted as "Holy Grail" but can also be interpreted as "Royal Blood" or the royal bloodline ("royal" referring to our bloodline). These people claim our bloodline was truly the Holy Grail.

These are some of the ideas that have been championed in the past—viewing the Holy Grail as a physical object, as Mary Magdalene herself, or as our "royal" (or sacred or holy) bloodline. None of these ideas have ever been proven, in the sense of someone being able to say definitively that one is the correct interpretation or the actual thing that happened. Rather, they are stories that speak strongly to people, stories that refuse to die, like so many of the things surrounding me, and surrounding Mary Magdalene, too. There is a certain potency or power in the story itself.

There is one more way that the term "Holy Grail" is used in your world. People sometimes refer to being on a quest or to a particular attainment being "the Holy Grail" of whatever is being sought. Such a reference is understood as an analogy for searching for something unique and valuable, something that will have great importance and significance, and which could make a great change. That is an interpretation I resonate with.

Yeshua: Now I would like to share how Mary Magdalene and I view the Holy Grail. What I want to communicate is extremely profound and far-reaching, but that may not be apparent at first. It may take time for this understanding to filter through constructs that already exist, either for you individually or for your world at the collective level. It has already taken a great deal of time for humans to even be available to hear this.

The story that the Holy Grail was my beloved Mary Magdalene is accurate in some ways, but the true meaning of that is generally not fully grasped. You see, Mary and I incarnated together as twin flames[11] or eternal beloveds. The work we came to do was mutual work. It was not just me coming as the Christ[12] or the Messiah[13] or the Son of God.[14] It was Mary *and* me coming as the Divine Feminine *and* the Divine Masculine,[15] in union with each other.

We came into a world that was not at all prepared for us coming together as the Divine Feminine and Masculine. Our mission was to shift that. We came to shift the course of humanity, to not only be open to us in divine union but to celebrate that. This required the world to shift into celebrating the Feminine.[16] That was very radical for that time.

You see, humans incarnated into the Earth realm with a very particular mission. You all have your individual missions or soul paths.[17] But beyond your personal or individual mission, you also incarnated with a collective mission. *That collective mission was to embrace the Feminine.*

I must explain what it means to embrace the Feminine. Mary has already done this beautifully, especially through her messages that are recorded in the book *Mary Magdalene Beckons*. So I am simply recapping what she has much more fully expressed.

To embrace the Feminine is to embrace *all* manifestation as God. It means to embrace the Earth as Sacred Feminine. It means to embrace your physical body as the form and temple of God, the manifestation of God itself. It means to embrace your sexuality as sacred—an expression of God and a way of moving to higher planes and frequencies of communion with God. It is to embrace your emotions as guides to God—both your joyful emotions *and* your painful emotions. It means to become a master of the energy world. And through all of these ways, to live in your heart and express your divinity as love. All of that is embracing the Feminine. And all those forms of embracing the Feminine are what human beings came to experience in this realm and place called Earth.

I am not speaking to just this lifetime. All of you have lived on Earth for many lifetimes. So I am speaking to a vast progression of lifetimes.

Before ever coming to Earth, you existed in what can be described as the transcendent state or the transcendent form of God. This transcendent state is prior to manifestation. It is what many of you experience when you meditate, that sense of a vast ocean of peace. Sometimes you call it "the Infinite" or "the Eternal," because it is outside of space and time. It is the realm of pure consciousness. Some of your religions and spiritual paths are especially focused on reaching this state of oneness beyond manifestation, often emphasizing meditation as a means for realizing this state.

I refer to this transcendental state, prior to manifestation, as the Masculine side of God. And I say to you, that is where you came from.

You came here to Earth to know something different. You didn't come here to know the unmanifest God, prior to manifestation. You came here to know God *in form, in manifestation.* That is the Feminine side of God.

Neither the Masculine nor the Feminine side of God will fulfill you when it is isolated or cut off from the other. Only the union of the Masculine and Feminine will truly fulfill you.

You came to Earth to embrace the Feminine. You actually came here to be leaders in the cosmic unfolding, the cosmic dance you might say, which has fathomless parts to it. The human part of that dance has everything to do with manifesting the Feminine and embracing that manifestation. This means embracing your physicality, your emotions, your sexuality, and Mother Earth. It means being the leaders of what it is to stand in love, as love, through your embrace of the Feminine.

But that's not what happened for most human beings. Most human beings (for most of history) went into shock when they manifested in this Earth realm. You suddenly felt disconnected from your prior connection to God in the Masculine transcendent form, and you were scared. Suddenly, you were facing the possibility of mortality and suffering, and you forgot your mission.

Human beings have been on a long journey of trying to control this frightening place. The control you drew upon was that of the Masculine controlling the Feminine. This has taken many forms. Many of you, and especially those who are listening to this communication, are very aware of your history of the Masculine controlling the Feminine. Yet I say that for most, you have much more to learn. You do not realize how internalized this control of the Feminine has become and how cut off most of you still are—men and women—from the Feminine.

Simply look to your relationship with your bodies, your emotions, and your sexuality. Look to your challenges with love. Look to how the Earth is getting treated at this time. In all these arenas you will see the signs of your still being unconscious of the Feminine and your present-time refusal to fully embrace the Feminine.

Mary Magdalene and I came together to change the course of history on Earth. We came to turn your path away from fear, blaming, and cutting away the Feminine. We came to change all of that to one of love, specifically love of the Feminine. Yet this is not what got recorded in your history, either your church history or any other form of history. Instead, the Feminine was still looked at as the enemy, and every attempt was made to cut the Feminine out of my story.

So, you have a Church that excluded women, a Church that claimed me to be celibate and cut off from women, born of a woman who had no sexuality and was cut off from her own Feminine. A Church that espoused a Father God cut off from a Mother God, claiming that I was the Son of God, as opposed to Child of God, or that Mary Magdalene and I were Son and Daughter. And Mary Magdalene was cut out of the story altogether, except to make her so small and to dismiss her as unworthy because she was associated with sexuality, in the hope that she would have no power. There is truth in the part that she was associated with sexuality, as was I. [Yeshua laughs.] Sexuality is part of our divinity, not sin, not anything that needs to be repented of. I have sadness about the tremendous distortion that was recorded and passed on.

But there was the Grail. And the Grail was the part that could not be controlled. It was the secret, the truth that would not die, the truth of the Feminine and my love of the Feminine. I am only empowered when I am embracing the Feminine. That is the path I modeled, and that is the path I call all of you to embrace as well.

The Holy Grail is the Feminine. You have a marvelous painting that relates to the King Arthur legend, showing Queen Guinevere knighting one of the knights.[18] He is bowing before her on one knee as she knights him with a sword. A great deal of wisdom is expressed through this painting. It shows the Masculine submitting, surrendering, and deferring to the Feminine. And through that, the Masculine receives the blessing of the Feminine, coming through the sword and empowering the Masculine.

The Accolade by Edmund Blair Leighton

You see, the Masculine cannot be empowered without the blessing and love of the Feminine. *The empowered Masculine leads through loving the Feminine.* The Masculine initiates through protecting, caring for, and loving the Feminine. Through that the Feminine empowers the Masculine. Then they are united and wholly prepared in their full power to serve and to love. That is the mystery of the Grail, and it is absolutely holy.

Yeshua: You may be wondering, *What does this have to do with me now and with our world?*

It has everything to do with your world! Some of your artists, perhaps going back to the 1960s, were very tuned into this. "All you need is love."[19] It may sound simple, yet as most of you know, it's not easy. The reason it's not easy is because you have not done the foundational work.

You must return to your roots relative to the Feminine. From an early age, most of you were taught not to feel and express emotions that might disturb people. This is especially true for boys. If boys cry or express fear, what are they called? They're told that they're being "a girl," and nothing could be worse. What is that communicating? It's communicating hatred of the Feminine. As boys get older, they're called other names that refer to the Feminine as something to be abhorred and avoided at all costs. And then they're told they're supposed to be a super-lover, but that mostly means performing. It doesn't really mean love.

Girls also get messages not to feel or show emotions—not to be too sensitive, not to be an angry "you know what." What's more, girls have gotten the message that if they want to succeed in the world and be anything more than unpaid servants, they need to go into their Masculine. Because of this, women have become very skillful at going into their Masculine and have accomplished much in the Masculine world, which is mostly your business world. Yet many of these women suffer by not having the love in their life that they want, or being stressed out, or having a feeling of emptiness because they miss the Feminine.

I have such sadness about this, such mourning. I want everyone to know the love of the Feminine that I know with my beloved Mary Magdalene. I want *her* love, *her* greatness, and *her* magnificence to be recognized, experienced, celebrated, and treasured by all, the way that so many have chosen to relate to me. You must understand that I am not empowered without Mary. The stories you were told came through the filter of those who were deeply afraid of the Feminine.

But this is shifting now in your world. You are at a time where there is new awareness. Women are finding their voice. They are speaking of how their Feminine has been transgressed in some of the grossest ways. It is vitally important that this be expressed. Out of this, men (and humanity altogether, but in particular men) are starting to awaken to the fact that something's off in their relationship to women. Something's off in relationship to what it is to be a man and how to be a man. Something's off in relationship to the world altogether. This is a hopeful sign.

What is off is that humanity does not yet know the Feminine, by and large.

This is the discovery of the Holy Grail.

Yeshua: Many of you want to know, *How do I find this? Where do I go? What are my next steps?* I say to you, "Go within."

The Grail literally lives within each one of you. It is the sacred chalice within all of you. The Grail is part of your light body or energetic grid. It's located within your brain core. And it is accessed through the awakening of the *Kundalini*.[20]

Some of you have heard of Kundalini and know it has something to do with the spine. Perhaps you've heard it's a serpent energy that's coiled at the base of the spine and which moves up the spine when it's activated.

Some of you have been told the Kundalini is dangerous, that it can hurt you if it becomes activated when you're not fully prepared or not being guided by someone who understands how to navigate the awakened Kundalini. There is some accuracy to this. But by and large, the Kundalini is a natural, safe process. It is a necessary part of your transition beyond the third dimension into the higher states of consciousness and higher dimensions of being.

It is valuable to find a teacher who can guide you in the process of Kundalini. But even before finding such a teacher, you must do the foundation work, which will make you ready, prepared, and safe to awaken the Kundalini. That foundation work is what Mary Magdalene has outlined so clearly and accurately. It is the foundation work relative to your body, sexuality, and emotions.

Mary has shared superbly what you must do to be mature and complete in the arenas of your body, sexuality, and emotions. She has stated, and I wholeheartedly agree, that of those three arenas (body, sexuality, and emotions), the one that the majority of you need the most is relative to emotions. Opening to your emotions and learning the skills for allowing your emotions to guide you into God-connection is the necessary preparation for awakening your energy body and Kundalini. This will lead you to the Grail and to living as love in your heart.

You might have moments, experiences, glimpses, or tastes of the energy body, or Kundalini, or of living in your heart. But until you do the foundation work, you will not be able to shift into that being your stable, ongoing state. You won't be able to maintain that awakening and love. You will not be able to live as that. You must do the foundation work first. And for most of you, that involves love of your emotions.

When you do that foundational work, followed by the energy work, and are able to locate the Grail within yourself, then you can also open to the Grail in relationship. This occurs through your sexuality, your energetic sharing with another. You can experience the "Grail of Union" with another being, which is not only a magnificent experience and a tremendous joy but also a great spiritual boon and support, if approached rightly.

All of this will lead you into transforming yourself and your world into a literal Garden of Eden,[21] where the serpent is your activated Kundalini, and you are unashamed of your nakedness. Rather, you celebrate your human form as the exquisite creation of God that it is. And you celebrate the union of Feminine and Masculine, which you came here to Earth to manifest, to champion, to be a cosmic leader for. This is the Grail quest to which I call all of you and for which I am the way shower.

When you know this path, when you discover the Grail, you will have the great bliss of communion with Mother-Father-God. I invoke this bliss of communion for all of you, for yourselves and your collective. I invoke it for your expression of humanity manifesting on Earth and through Earth for all the cosmos.

Come join me there. We await you.

Mary Magdalene: My beloved Yeshua has spoken about loving the Feminine. He is a consummate master of such love.

The Masculine loves the Feminine through bringing consciousness[22] and by creating a container of love for the Feminine.[23] Then the Feminine can shine her radiance through the essence of her being—to her beloved, to all of her beloveds, and to the world altogether. That is the function of the Feminine, to share her radiance.[24]

There are many ways to be the radiance of the Feminine. One of the key ways is through expressing and showing emotions. This is not the same as what is sometimes called "acting out" or "dramatizing" emotions. This is not the same as hurting people with emotions, not at all. This is vulnerably expressing your emotional life, becoming transparent and showing your emotions. Yet, as my beloved Yeshua expressed, many of you were trained *not* to do this from an early age and thus to deny the Feminine. You were trained that if you want to be accepted, you need to go into your mind, which is the domain of the Masculine.

Many of you have spent the majority of your life in your mind. What we are talking about is a way of loving the Feminine through journeying out of your mind, literally, and into your heart. You do that through feeling rather than thinking. Then you share that feeling in the world.

The Feminine and the Masculine are not the same. All of you contain both. Yet most of you will lean toward one or the other. Those who identify as the female gender will tend to lean toward the Feminine. Those who identify as the male gender will tend to lean toward the Masculine. But all of you need access to both, and for many of you this will require the kind of strengthening of the Feminine I've described.

The Feminine is about vulnerability. It is about love. And love is an equal power to consciousness. They are the great beloveds of each other.

If you wish to celebrate me,[25] what I ask and call you to is to celebrate love—specifically love of the Feminine. Love your Earth. Love your physical body. Love your sexuality. Love your emotions. You will know it is true love if it opens your heart, if it leads you into union with the ultimate beloved, who is God.

Most of you will need help in this process because you have not learned the skills of loving the Feminine. You will need help to release the wrong adaptations you have assumed and learn the skills that truly support you. I urge you to make use of the help that Mercedes offers,[26] just as Yeshua and I are doing our utmost to support you.

Love has already won. Yet humans must still do their part. Transformation is required for this love to blossom in your world. We support that transformation to the best of our ability as we watch the unfolding process, knowing that love will win and it is not a competition.

In the great light of consciousness, the great love of the heart, we bless you and love you. We hold you now and always in love and light.

PART II
HIGHER MASCULINE AND FEMININE

TWO

CHRIST CONSCIOUSNESS

Yeshua: I would like to speak about Christ consciousness, for I believe that not everyone understands what this is.

I will begin with the term "Christ." This term does not refer to any particular being, religion, or spiritual path. The word "Christ" has been used by the religion of Christianity, and because of that many associate the term with that religion. But *I* do not make this association, nor does Mary. "Christ" is a reference to carrying the light of God. In your world of manifestation, light is the closest form to pure consciousness.

You could view the realm of manifestation as a spectrum. On one end of the spectrum are the things that are completely involved in manifestation. On the other end is what transcends manifestation. Within this spectrum, light is the closest to what transcends manifestation. Christ consciousness is the purest light—the light of Creator. And Christ is the carrier of that light.

When I incarnated two thousand years ago, my purpose was to bring that light into your world and consciousness. I did so to support all of you in connecting with that light, so you could become carriers of that light. Ultimately, you will realize *you* are the light. *Everything* is that light. All is Christ consciousness.

Christ consciousness resides in the transcendent, prior to manifestation. That "place" is limitless, infinite, eternal, beyond time and space. Your spiritual and religious traditions have called this transcendental realm various names, such as the "pure Buddha land," "beyond the beyond," "the Self," "heaven," and "the Father." Some of those names have taken on interpretations and meanings other than the purity of the transcendent. It is difficult to conceive of the transcendent within the framework of manifestation, since it is outside of manifestation. Yet the transcendent is absolutely real and is available to all of you.

The primary experience most people have when they connect with this transcendent place is peace. There is an expression many of you are familiar with: "The peace that surpasses all understanding." This is a reference to going beyond the mind, because consciousness is not the same as the mind.

The mind is part of manifestation. It is related to thinking and the brain. The mind has the ability to connect with consciousness, but the mind is not the same as consciousness.

Pure consciousness points to the divine light and even beyond, to the unknowable, the prior. Out of pure consciousness, the manifest is created.

Your story of Adam and Eve points to this. Eve being created from Adam's rib is an allegory for the Divine Feminine of manifestation being created out of the Divine Masculine of pure consciousness. In fact, your consciousness is always creating. You may not fully recognize this yet because in the third dimension a great deal of time often lapses between creation and its manifestation in your world. But it is definitely the case that you are always creating out of consciousness.

The creation of form originally came out of pure consciousness. This is why manifestation is not ultimately different from consciousness.

This oneness is expressed in the formula of your great scientist, Einstein, who said $E = mc^2$. There's a relationship between energy, matter, and light, but ultimately, they're all the same. They're just different forms. So it is with the beloved Feminine and Masculine.

I am speaking to the part of you that is already consciousness, even if you don't yet know it or realize it. You can't be other than consciousness. Through your spiritual process you are more and more coming to realize and understand that consciousness.

Consciousness is not a belief or an idea to be held in your mind. You certainly can hold it as a belief, but doing so will not benefit you very much. It might even be a blockage to your spiritual growth. Consciousness is something you will *realize*. When you realize it, you will know that realization has occurred because your manifestation changes. It changes who you are at the core of your being.

Some spiritual paths have devoted themselves to attaining and living this pure consciousness, particularly in India, Tibet, China, Japan, and Asia in general. These spiritual paths have developed many practices for helping people attain the realization of consciousness. However, many of these consciousness traditions have not equally embraced the Feminine, and this has caused problems in your world. When you deny the Feminine, it does not ultimately support you.

There may be times when you choose to focus on consciousness exclusively, such as in meditation. That can be very valuable. But such times need to be balanced with engaging the divine in Feminine form.

This is your great challenge in your world at this time. There has been such a focus on the Masculine, while excluding the Feminine, that even your spiritual practices often don't help you, and at times they even hinder you.

Similarly, when the Feminine is embraced in your world, it is often divorced from the Divine Masculine and the bringing of the light of consciousness. The Feminine then is embraced at a lower frequency or even in a debased form. This has caused some people to conclude that the Feminine is the problem. But the Feminine is never the problem. Nor is the Masculine. They both must be understood as manifestations of the divine and lived in their highest form and frequency, in their true relationship to each other of love and union.

I wish to add one more thing. Many of you have images of spiritual beings, such as the Buddha or me. These images often convey the quality of consciousness visually, including great peace, timelessness, and spaciousness, prior to manifestation. Such images may be helpful for you as another way of connecting to, understanding, and ultimately discovering this consciousness within and as yourself.

Mary Magdalene: My guess is that most of you resonate with the term "Christ consciousness"; it has meaning for you. There is something attractive about the term, something that your soul responds to. It calls you to something that you know in your soul.

Yet if someone were to ask you, "What does Christ consciousness mean?", you may have a difficult time explaining it in a rational, conscious way. This does not mean that the concept is not meaningful. It simply means that your connection to Christ consciousness is coming from somewhere other than your rational, thinking mind.

Christ consciousness has a lot to do with what Yeshua brought in his incarnation on Earth. He brought the embodiment of Christ consciousness into human form. Another way of saying this is that he embodied the light, because Christ consciousness brings the light. It's the part of us that recognizes and knows the light.

Light is a manifestation of God. It is one quality of God—a very important one. Yeshua embodied that light. This is why so many were attracted to him; they saw the light in him. It's why so many continue to be drawn to him. They see the light in him even beyond his physical human incarnation.

I can speak very personally that I see the light in Yeshua. To me he is the embodiment of light, however he manifests or comes to us. My heart responds because I, like most people, love the light.

THREE

MAGDALENE LOVE

Mary Magdalene: There is a complement to Christ consciousness—that attraction to light that draws so many beings to the spiritual path. The complement to Christ consciousness is *Magdalene love*. While most of you are familiar with the idea of Christ consciousness, it is likely you have not heard the term "Magdalene love." There is a reason for this.

At the time Yeshua and I incarnated, my part was to bring Magdalene love, as the complement to Yeshua bringing Christ consciousness. But the world was not ready for the embodiment of the Divine Feminine, and those in power did much to suppress my part.

Yet the suppression did not work. Ultimately, my part survived, just as an ember survives from a fire. It could not be extinguished because Magdalene love is part of reality. It can be denied, but that does not change its existence.

Now, at this time, there is a resurgence. Your world today is quite different and is ready to receive my part, which brings me great joy. It is as though the flame is being fanned once again.

A growing movement is underway—a groundswell of those who are responding in some form or another to Mary Magdalene, which is as it should be. It is a rebalancing, a returning to the whole, a calling back of the part that was denied, that those in power tried to remove and cut away. Magdalene love is being brought back.

What do I mean by Magdalene love? You have a sense of what love is. You experience love in your life in many different ways. Magdalene love is the totality or wholeness of all the ways human beings have the capacity for love. Love is the complement to light. Together, love and light are the basis of all reality.

What is the difference between love and light? This is a bit theoretical. I hope you are able to stay with me through this. We will get more practical shortly.

At their core or essence, love and light relate to the two primary aspects of the divine. The concept of the divine having two parts is still unfamiliar for many of you, so I shall briefly review that understanding.

Originally, there was only God, and God was all there is. You could call this God undifferentiated *Source*. At some point, there was a movement within God, or the divine, to know itself in form, in manifestation. That was the beginning of the *descension process*,[27] of God manifesting itself in form.

The first step of this process was the manifestation into Mother-Father God. You might think of this as a single cell starting to grow. The initial growth is to divide itself into two parts—Mother God and Father God. Out of this initial division came more manifestation in increasingly lower frequencies of matter or form. This created the dimensions, starting with the highest dimensions and going progressively lower and lower until reaching the third dimension, which is the dimension you find yourselves in now.

This process of descension, of moving from pure Source into lower and lower dimensions until you came to the place where you are currently, was all part of the process of God knowing itself in embodiment, form, manifestation. You all came through this process of descension, so you all carry these original two parts of the descension process. It's a blueprint, carried within, of Mother-Father God in the form of Sacred Masculine and Divine Feminine.

These parts of you carry different qualities and purposes. Each has an exalted part, which is the part that is most connected to that original seed, that first step down into manifestation that created Mother-Father God. For the Sacred Masculine, that highest part is consciousness. Light is another way of referring to that part. In its purity, light refers to highest consciousness or Christ consciousness.

All of you carry that light. And you carry a longing to fulfill that light in its highest form of Christ consciousness. It's a movement toward the highest. Sometimes this is referred to as "doing good," but I prefer to look at it as doing what is for the highest. "Good" is often confined to a third-dimensional, dualistic concept of good versus bad, and it also is often associated with rules of what is and isn't good. Christ consciousness is not limited by those kinds of third-dimensional ideas. It is neither rule oriented nor dualistic. It is for the highest, which is always in the present, clear, and unique to each moment.

You also have another part, which is your Divine Feminine. In its highest frequency and calling, the Divine Feminine manifests as love. *Love is pure consciousness in action.*

At the time Yeshua and I incarnated, I embodied as the carrier of the Divine Feminine, in service to her. My role and unique soul calling was to bring forth love. And it was in relationship to Yeshua. Together we represented the wholeness of love-light. This wholeness reflects the nature of God, because God is both. God is light or pure consciousness. And God is love.

You are all carriers of both light and love, perhaps not in its fullness or completion, but there is no question that you all carry the potential for that wholeness within yourself. The spiritual path is to realize that wholeness of light and love—as yourself, as God, and as all of manifestation.

We came to help all in understanding, turning to, and realizing that light and love. But love is a challenging thing. You could say that the Feminine is challenging in many ways. [Mary laughs.] So love is also challenging.

While many of you like the idea of love (as a concept) and even long to embody love, you are also challenged by love. This is because love makes you vulnerable. Love is an opening of your being. Through that opening, you become vulnerable to pain. Vulnerability to pain is the great challenge of the human condition. This is the primary arena that humans in general are growing in. Opening to love is your spiritual work. And in that opening there is skill to know how to navigate the pain that love opens you to.

I have spoken a great deal about this, how in opening yourself to love you must open yourself to pain. Part of knowing love in this realm is to love pain and to trust it, to know that it is there to help you, which indeed it is. This is not to say that it's easy, nor to deny that it's painful. It may be emotionally painful, physically painful, or painful in other ways. But this is part of the human experience. Part of knowing love in this realm is to open to pain and to let that pain grow you. Pain grows you into greater love.

This is not a philosophy that you should try to be in as much pain as you possibly can because that's going to benefit you the most. Rather, it is that you should be in the most love that you can, and with that will inevitably come pain in this realm. Learn to open to that pain and to love that part too. And love yourself in the midst of pain (which means to care for yourself) without denying or running away from the pain. Open your heart to pain as your great help in uniting with God in this realm, and certainly your great help in opening to love.

As you do that, you will know love, and you will know light. You will know the great joy, bliss, and ecstasy of love, as I have known with my beloved Yeshua.

Your destiny is to be in love all the time, held in the light. This is the path and the calling for all of you. It is the reality that you will inevitably know as you follow this path.

FOUR

God as Masculine *and* Feminine

Mary Magdalene: Many of you hear the word "God" as meaning Masculine, which it does not. It means the Masculine *and* Feminine divine. Of course, it is just a word, and everyone relates to words differently. Nevertheless, if you have been programmed to relate to God as Masculine, then when you hear the word "God," you will likely think of a Masculine being.

God is neither Masculine nor Feminine. It is also true that God is *completely* Masculine and *completely* Feminine. All of those statements are true, and there is no conflict between any of them. As you evolve in your spiritual consciousness, this will become increasingly clear and simple to you. We hope to help you with this understanding because this understanding is an important part of the ascension process.[28]

FIVE

EXALTED MASCULINE

Yeshua: The Masculine and Feminine both have a more practical and a more exalted manifestation.

For the Masculine, the more practical aspect involves mental clarity and using the mind to accomplish things. This part of the Masculine engages the practical aspects of mind, which you might call your lower or thinking mind. The practical Masculine also involves engaging the will, which means engaging power and a kind of force. The practical Masculine harnesses energy, will, and mind to accomplish things. It establishes, pursues, and accomplishes goals.

The exalted aspect of the Masculine is consciousness. You could think of this as living in the mind of God and being God's will.

In your world, the Masculine has tended to manifest in practical forms. Your world has become very mentally based and focused on power and force, while excluding, discounting, and denying other ways of relating to reality. As you grow in your spiritual process, this will change. You will more and more become the exalted

Masculine, resting as consciousness and abiding as the will of God. This is a form of Christ consciousness, of being a carrier of light.

It is optimal for individuals to be fully connected to both the practical and exalted forms of the Masculine, such that Christ consciousness can direct the functional or practical Masculine.

Your world today is largely being directed by the consciousness of the third dimension, which is a much lower frequency than Christ consciousness. Third-dimensional consciousness is centered upon survival, based on the idea that you die. It also involves duality or the idea that reality is made up of opposing forces. Two of the biggest dualistic concepts in your world are the ideas of right-wrong and good-bad.

These ideas create an overriding sense that your survival is at stake. Reality is seen as *life versus death*, and life is fueled by a struggle to survive and maintain life, which is the "good" or "desirable" pole of duality. Similarly, you have to work against the "bad" pole of duality, which is death. For example, you have doctors saying "we won the battle" when someone lives, or "we lost the battle" when someone dies. This is one small example, but this consciousness is woven into your thoughts, beliefs, and motivations. A great deal of your life is devoted to staying vigilant, so you're always on the pole of staying alive and avoiding the pole of dying.

This "battle" to stay alive and fend off death is what the practical Masculine is devoted to, based upon third-dimensional, dualistic consciousness.

In Christ consciousness, you cannot be separated from light and life. You cannot lose it. You may change your form, which is all that death is, but you do not vanish or suddenly cease to exist. Once you are fully connected to Christ consciousness, you never lose your connection to light, in whatever form it manifests. You do not come from a place of struggle, of fighting to achieve one pole of duality and avoid the other pole.

Other aspects of Christ consciousness are also different from third-dimensional consciousness and reality. In the third dimension, a great deal of what you experience and learn has to do with power: *What is power? What are the effects of power? What does it feel like to have power or not to have power? How is power handled between and amongst people? What is the relationship between power and love, power and light?*

In your practical Masculine—not directed by Christ consciousness—you see the effects of power in many ways. You see power struggles—power used for conflict or competition. There is an assumption that only some will have power, that there will be winners and losers in the power game.

In Christ consciousness, power is always in service to the divine; it always serves light and love. This form of power supports, blesses, and unites. You still may choose to employ the practical Masculine aspects, but they will be in service to Christ consciousness. So, rather than duality, you are operating out of oneness. Rather than power-over or power-against, you're operating out of power-with.

Ultimately you will never understand this with your mind. It must be experienced. When you have the experience, there will be no question. It is unmistakable.

SIX

EXALTED FEMININE

Mary Magdalene: Just as there are different forms of the Masculine, there are also different forms of the Feminine. The practical form of the Feminine is simply manifestation. You experience this most obviously as physical manifestation. But there are other forms of manifestation. Energy is a form of manifestation, which has a higher frequency. If you slowed energy down, it would most likely become a physical manifestation. Similarly, emotions are a form of manifestation with their own frequency. Thoughts are also a form of manifestation when they come into your mind as an idea. These are all aspects of the Feminine.

In the Feminine's exalted form, the highest quality is love.

You experience love in your body, your energy, your emotions, and you recognize it. For many of you, your first experiences of love were of your immediate family—your mother, father, or others in your family. This expanded throughout your life to become love of others and love of God, in whatever form you experience

God. Ultimately, all love is love of God. It is loving God in a particular form or manifestation.

All activities of love are what we are calling "Magdalene love." They are the manifestation of the divine, God, spirit, or whatever word you want to use, in the form of love. It is the complement to the Masculine. The Feminine is in life, in manifestation, where the Masculine is beyond, pure, prior. Calling the exalted form of the Feminine "Magdalene love" is a means of pointing to all as God.

Our hope is that referring to the exalted Masculine as Christ consciousness and the exalted Feminine as Magdalene love also connects you with the exceedingly powerful connection and union between Yeshua and me—between the carrier of light and the manifestation of love. We hope this helps people in your world realize the union of these different forms of the divine—the union of the purity of consciousness in its transcendental form and the ecstasy and perfection of love in manifest form.

You tend to see spirituality as being either about love or transcendence. You don't necessarily see it as both, in union. Yet there have been traditions and individuals who have understood and realized the union of love and transcendence. This union is where you are all headed. Ultimately, you can never divorce yourself from one or the other. Both are your nature, in union with each other.

This is what we have come to support in all.

SEVEN

EMBRACING THE FEMININE AS BELOVED

Yeshua: The Masculine has used the mind and power to create a situation where the Feminine is suppressed, and the Masculine dominates. This is not the nature of Christ consciousness. Christ consciousness recognizes the Feminine as the beloved and as itself. The nature of Christ consciousness is union.

When I said, "Love your neighbor as yourself," many people took that as a prescription for how to relate *to another*. At its highest level, "as yourself" literally means your neighbor *is* yourself. All manifestation is *yourself*, only. There is only one. This is the higher form. This is the form you are moving into. And it will be *very* different from the way the Masculine has tended to manifest in your world.

Your embrace of the Feminine will be one of your greatest supports for transitioning into the higher Masculine. Even now those manifested as males often realize that it is through uniting with a female that they are able to be their best version of themselves. This is not to say that everyone must have a partner if they want to evolve. Once again, it is a picture, an allegory. Everything is complete, in whatever form, if you realize it as such.

EIGHT

YESHUA AND MARY MAGDALENE AS MODELS

Mary Magdalene: It does not matter to us to be remembered as we incarnated on Earth two thousand years ago, or that you hold onto a story of us from our incarnation. Instead, feel *through* the story to the meaning of our incarnation and the work that we are dedicated to. What we care about most is our present-time help for you in *your* growth, so you may become what we demonstrated. Yeshua has said the same. It was always his clarity and purpose *not* to be worshiped or set aside as unique, although all of us are unique. As he was recorded to say, "All this and more shall *you* do."[29]

We came to model the path of connecting with God for you. We are *still* modeling this for you. We do not wish to be worshiped. We do not wish to be set aside as something different from you or held to a particular form. Do not limit us to our incarnation and story from two thousand years ago. The importance was the work we did to support and guide you. We didn't come for you to focus on us but for you to receive our gifts of help. That is still what we wish.

Our greatest desire and joy is to support and celebrate the Divine Feminine and Masculine *as you, in you, through you,* and also manifesting in everything—in complete, utter, ecstatic union with each other. With that understanding, we're happy for you to hold us as models, bearers, gift givers, supporters, and lovers of the Divine Feminine in union with the Divine Masculine.

NINE

Yeshua and Mary Magdalene as Complements

Yeshua: My beloved Mary Magdalene and I often take the roles of the Divine Masculine and the Divine Feminine in relation to each other. It's natural and joyful for us to do this, even as we both are fully connected to our own Masculine and Feminine within. It is our choice and our joy to rest in these complementary positions—where I hold the space of pure consciousness in relation to Mary as she holds the space of manifestation in relation to me.

At these times, it is often natural (for both of us) for Mary to be the one who speaks as I rest in consciousness and send my blessing from that space. I certainly will speak if there is anything I wish to contribute or add.

Mary has my full blessings to communicate for both of us. I am so grateful for her brilliance, her wisdom, and her amazing ability to communicate with all. I recognize and honor her to the highest degree for her service to all beings. She is quite the adept, especially at helping people with the more practical aspects before you.

Mary Magdalene: I also honor and recognize my beloved Yeshua with my fullest heart-love and deepest gratitude. I am so grateful for his presence in my life and in all manifestations. I am grateful for the blessing that he brings, which is so immense, so huge.

Yeshua's work in manifestation was a tremendous surrendering to his spiritual calling. What he did to manifest in the third dimension, and then to teach in physical form in the way that he did, is something that all of you will come to understand increasingly over time. You will understand what that required and the miracle that it was. I simply wish to acknowledge that miracle and to once again bow down in love to my beloved Yeshua, who has served all beings so incredibly and continues to do so.

PART III

THE JOURNEY

TEN

YOUR HIGHER SELF

Yeshua: From the Masculine point of view, nothing is more wonderful than abiding as pure consciousness. Yet ultimately there is absolutely no difference between the pure Masculine of complete consciousness and the pure Feminine of absolute love. They are two sides of the mirror, two sides of the coin. You are always already both.

You have chosen to come into this manifest form where your consciousness is limited. Now your consciousness reflects the manifestation that you chose. However, part of you remembers something higher. That part of you is your *higher self*.[30] Your higher self is calling you to change your consciousness and, through that, to change your manifestation.

All are called. All are actually responding in their own way and their own form, which is right for them at this time. You can't help but do it. You *are* doing it.

Yet in the third dimension you have free will. Part of your journey in the third dimension is to engage your free will to support this wonderful process of uniting in and as God. It doesn't make sense to your mind. I recommend listening to your heart and your consciousness. Let those be your guide.

ELEVEN

Unconditional and Conditional Love

Mary Magdalene: All love is unconditional. What I mean is that love is never given in a conditional way. It is never given as a kind of a deal where "I will love you if you give me something back." That is not love. That is a contract. Contracts can be appropriate at certain times and in certain circumstances. It is just good to understand that that is not love.

Love is always given freely. When you fully love, you cannot help but *give* love. It is your great joy to give love. This is the meaning of unconditional love.

In your spiritual world there are some who have suggested a different concept of unconditional love. They propose that the highest, most spiritual love is impersonal or universal love. This kind of love is uniform and the same for all. It is then suggested that personal love, which some call "special love"—loving someone as special or different—is somehow not unconditional or true love and, therefore, is not the highest or most spiritual love. I would say this is misguided.

There are many different kinds of love. You will experience many different kinds of love in your lifetime if you open yourself to love. Not only is this completely natural, it is also intentional. You came into this realm because your soul desired and needed certain experiences for your soul growth.

All the different relationships in your life are what your soul has called in to support you in your growth by giving you the experiences that will most help you. Those relationships are unique. Some of them *are* special. You could say they are all special in a certain way because they are all important to you, your life, and your soul development. Your response to each relationship will be different. The way that you manifest love in each relationship will be different because your soul has called in that particular way of loving for your growth.

If you are called to love in a unique way in any given relationship, I suggest that you support that and open to it. Let love be your guide, and follow it. I do not recommend following what seems to me an artificial concept that you *shouldn't* feel a unique love for someone that's different from your love for others.

I certainly know special love in my being, and it is a great gift from God. I would not want to hold back from it. It does not in any way detract from my loving all in the more universal sense. Quite the opposite, it supports and grows my capacity for universal love. Every way that you know love is a divine gift, an opening to greater union with God. Do not hold back.

Yeshua was a great advocate of love. One of the things that was accurately recorded of his teaching was the admonition to love God with all your being and to love others as yourself. This is what he brought and who he was. He was a great lover of me and of so many. And his love for each of us was unique, personal, and completely divine.

Yet his primary role was to bring the light and, as the light, to be the container and holder of the Divine Feminine. My role was to be love and to bring love. Yeshua's light supported and held me in my manifestation of love. He did that perfectly.

To follow Christ consciousness is a wonderful thing. So is following the light. Yet it is not the wholeness. The light will inevitably bring you to love, just as love inevitably brings you to the light.

The most direct path, the path of wholeness, is to follow both. Follow the wholeness of light and love, of Christ consciousness and Magdalene love. This is the great path, the exceedingly powerful path. It is also the timely path right now for all of you as you move into the completion of your spiritual work in the third dimension and the beginning of your shift into the higher dimensions. Your work is to be the light and the love. Follow the light. Follow love.

TWELVE

Seeing the Higher Masculine and Feminine

Mary Magdalene: In your world, men are often attracted to youth and beauty in women. And women are often attracted to wealth and success in men. Yet many of you feel constrained by these images of Feminine and Masculine, and wish to go beyond the limitations they present.

The first thing I want to say is that the attributes you're referencing of beauty and youthfulness are wonderful things to be loved and enjoyed. In fact, when you transition into the fourth dimension (where the primary learning is about manifestation), one of the first and primary things you will all become adepts at is manifesting beauty and youth for yourself. [Mary laughs with enjoyment.] This is a wonderful practice. If you have the opportunity to connect with fourth-dimensional beings, you will notice that they are very beautiful and youthful because they have mastered the practice of manifestation.

In the third dimension, most people are not yet aware of their ability to manifest youth and beauty—or anything else for that matter. So, you are manifesting something different, by and large.

We recommend that you go beyond the limitation of *only* seeing the physical aspect of youth or beauty. Instead, see the heart and consciousness of the person. Let yourself be fed by the person's heart and consciousness, which are their exalted forms of Divine Feminine and Divine Masculine. What you will find when you do this is that these people will become beautiful to you. You may even see them as youthful. You are actually changing your manifestation through this practice of creation. Your reality will begin to change.

The same goes for seeing people as wealthy or successful. When you are seated in your heart and consciousness, you will begin to see the incredible wealth and success of every being you encounter. Just the fact that they have manifested in the Earth realm and are engaging their spiritual work here is a testament to the success of their spirituality. It's a testament to the success of the whole creation process, which you are all part of.

And there's incredible wealth in having so many beings manifested and bringing their qualities into your world. When you understand how everyone is a manifestation of God in human form and that they're bringing that God-manifestation to you in this moment, there's nothing more abundant and filled with wealth than that. As you all grow, this is what you will be experiencing more and more.

Part IV

Sacred Masculine in Life

THIRTEEN

Sacred Warrior

Yeshua: In your world, the archetype of the warrior is a role that many are familiar with and relate to. This archetype embodies qualities such as heroism, strength, and duty. These are valuable qualities that help to make individuals and societies successful.

There is a higher octave of the warrior, which I shall refer to as the sacred warrior. This is the version of the warrior that I am interested in. It is the spiritual aspect of the warrior and is very important for your spiritual development.

The primary quality of the sacred warrior is that he or she is guided by sacred purpose. This requires that you first know your sacred purpose, or soul purpose, and then that you are willing to follow it. Coming to know your soul purpose is often a quest in itself. Some of you know your soul purpose, even from a young age. Yet for others it is not clear. Becoming clear on your purpose is an important part of your spiritual journey. You can pray for the clarity you require, which I highly recommend.

It is possible that you are already connected with your soul purpose without realizing it. Soul purpose often manifests as something you feel strongly called to—something you feel motivated to engage, even without external support and sometimes with external challenges. Nonetheless, you're drawn to do that thing and pursue it as though internally driven. This is a sign of soul purpose.

A sacred warrior follows the call of his or her soul purpose, not for self-fulfillment but in service to God, spirit, and the greater good of all. This engagement of activity as service to God is another aspect of the sacred warrior. A sacred warrior feels his or her connection to God especially through the offering of deeds to support people's union with spirit. These deeds do not always have to be lofty. Often they are very practical things that support others in some way or other and, through that, free others up for their higher work or soul growth.

A sacred warrior follows a kind of sacred creed. This creed includes leaving the world a better place for all, living with honor, always doing your best, and being dependable and trustworthy.

Another aspect of the sacred warrior is engagement of self-discipline in service to achieving goals and mastering one's arena of service. An example of this is the monastic tradition, where great self-discipline is engaged as a means of uniting with God.

A sacred warrior has mastered his or her emotions so that he or she is not ruled by them. Anger is healed through forgiveness. Fear is overcome through service and submission to the higher. Sorrow is released through giving all to God.

A sacred warrior is a protector of all who are weaker, be they children, the sick, or the elderly. A sacred warrior is also a protector of the Feminine. The safety of others and the world is insured through the protection of the sacred warrior.

A sacred warrior is loyal to his or her sacred leaders and to his or her brother and sister sacred warriors. A sacred warrior cooperates, offering his or her skills for the good of all.

A sacred warrior supports life and light. He or she is living the admonition to love God with all one's strength. Sacred warriors are essential for all of you, as individuals, groups, and societies. It is the aspect in all of you that accomplishes things for the highest good.

Perhaps it is helpful to give a few examples of sacred warriors that you are likely familiar with. The knights of the round table, Native American warriors, and those who participated in the civil rights movement are but a few examples. A sacred warrior doesn't have to be one who does battle. It is one who puts his or her feet on the ground and shoulder to the wheel to get higher things done. There are probably many sacred warriors in your life right now, if you have eyes to see them.

Blessings to all of you as sacred warriors.

FOURTEEN

SACRED MAGICIAN

Yeshua: The sacred magician is another form that the Sacred Masculine can take in manifestation.

The sacred magician is about accessing the higher mind. Your higher mind is associated with the sixth chakra or third eye, whereas your lower or thinking mind is associated with the third chakra.

The sacred magician is able to connect with higher realms, states, and beings, and to bring back wisdom and guidance from these ascended places and beings. You see shamans and mystics doing this.

The sacred magician is also able to manifest through the higher mind. This aspect of the sacred magician has been expressed by some of your new age or progressive spiritual teachings, which speak about creating through your thoughts. The power of conscious creation is one of the primary focuses of learning and mastery in the fourth dimension.

The highest purpose of the sacred magician is to connect with pure consciousness—prior to space, time, and all arising.

Connecting with pure consciousness has been the focus of many eastern spiritual paths, often through the practice of meditation. The work of the sacred magician is to awaken higher consciousness and consciously create the highest reality.

Your present world is relatively developed in the practical Masculine aspects of both warrior and magician. Elevating these roles to their sacred octaves—of sacred warrior and sacred magician—is much of the foundational work in the third dimension. Mastery of these roles (of sacred warrior and sacred magician) is the necessary prerequisite for your further growth into the sacred lover and sacred king.

FIFTEEN

SACRED LOVER

Yeshua: It is time to speak of the sacred lover. This is a very important aspect of the Sacred Masculine for all of you. It is the frontier of human evolution at this time. And it's the biggest part of what you incarnated on Earth to learn about, through all your incarnations. It's also a great deal of what I incarnated for—to demonstrate and to teach.

The sacred lover is associated with the heart chakra. You might think of it as opening to the power of love. It also is very much about opening to the Feminine.

The sacred lover rests on the foundation of the sacred warrior and sacred magician. It is optimal that these foundational aspects of the Sacred Masculine (the sacred warrior and sacred magician) be already developed and strong to support the sacred lover. Then the sacred lover comes from a place of strength of body and mind. This strength is important because the sacred lover is about vulnerability and opening. It takes strength to do this. One who loves truly is strong.

The sacred aspect of the lover involves, first and foremost, love of God. I instructed you to love God with all your heart, soul, mind, and strength. All one's faculties are to be turned to God and utilized and employed for loving God. This is my primary admonition for how to live and how to be the sacred lover.

The second part of this admonition is to love your neighbor as yourself. Thus, the second part of being the sacred lover is to be love in relation to all manifest beings.

These two instructions together are the most important guidelines for all at the third-dimensional level.

There are three primary qualities of the sacred lover. The first is presence. This is a function of awareness and, ultimately, of consciousness. The sacred lover is fully present. This means being 100 percent devoted with your full attention to whatever is before you, rather than being distracted and away in one's mind, focused on other things. The practice of meditation can be a support for developing the ability to be fully present.

The second quality of the sacred lover is openness to the Feminine, which includes being connected to and expressive of one's inner Feminine. This openness requires that you respect and trust the Feminine. If you have past wounds in relation to the Feminine, you will need to heal those wounds in order to allow this openness. This openness to the Feminine is the part of the sacred lover that requires the most strength.

The third quality of the sacred lover is creating a container of support for the Feminine. This is different from the protection of the sacred warrior, which comes from a sense of duty to the highest good. The container created by the sacred lover is motivated by love and comes from the heart. You might actually see it as a circle of love, encircling the beloved.

When all three of these qualities are activated—presence, openness to the Feminine, and creating a circle of love and support for the Feminine—then the Feminine gives her gifts of wisdom, aliveness, feeling, love, energy, sexuality, and nurturing.

I demonstrated the sacred lover in my relationship with God, my followers, and with Mary Magdalene. Even though my sacred love relationship with Mary Magdalene was largely excluded from the record of my life and teaching, it still lives, and many are awakening to the truth of that relationship at this time. Our relationship is a model for all of you in incarnating the role of sacred lover.

May you be fully supported in your mastery of the role of sacred lover and know its bounteous fruits, which are a great treasure.

SIXTEEN

SACRED KING

Yeshua: I return again to speak about the sacred king.

The sacred king is the culmination of the other three Masculine archetypes of sacred warrior, magician, and lover—drawing on the qualities and strengths of each of these sacred archetypes and integrating them into the whole that becomes the sacred king. In addition, the sacred king adds the dimension of leadership to the three previous foundational archetypes.

The sacred king is associated with the seventh chakra, which is also known as the crown chakra. This is the chakra of integration of all the chakras, bridging them to what is higher. Thus, this chakra "crowns" the individual as king and sacred leader of all one's parts. Your inner Masculine is destined to become sacred king of yourself and to act from the role of sacred king in the world.

The sacred king can also appear as a leader of others. This could be as the "head" of a family, a manager or leader in a business or other organization, a political leader or head of state, or a spiritual leader. Some of the historical sacred kings you may be familiar with are me (as Jesus), Buddha, Moses, and the legend of King Arthur. More contemporary examples of sacred kings in your world are Mahatma Gandhi, the Dalai Lama, Martin Luther King Jr., and Mother Theresa.

The most important quality that exemplifies a sacred king is that he or she is committed to carrying out God's will for the greatest good of all. In doing so, he or she creates a "kingdom of God" on Earth. This is not a conventional kingdom, though it might also correspond to such. For example, the current Dalai Lama has no geographic area that he leads. Rather, the sacred king is primarily a leader of a spiritual kingdom—holding to, aligning with, and manifesting the highest values of spirit. The "head" of this kingdom includes all and draws upon the strengths of all, for the highest welfare of all.

This is a great calling for humanity and especially the Sacred Masculine. It is what the Sacred Masculine is evolving into and will be manifesting more and more over time. In the future, individuals will be strong in their inner sacred king, and groups will choose to be unified and led by sacred kings. That will be a wonderful time for your Earth. It will also be one of the signs of your readiness to move into the fourth dimension. May the manifestation of the sacred king within all come soon, for the sake of all.

So shall it be.

PART V

DIVINE FEMININE IN LIFE

SEVENTEEN

FEMININE–MASCULINE DIFFERENCES

Mary Magdalene: I come to you today to talk about the difference between the Sacred Masculine and the Divine Feminine. Some of you may wonder why these terms are different. Why not "Sacred Feminine" or "Divine Masculine"?

The more superficial response to this question is that the terms most commonly used in your culture today are Sacred Masculine and Divine Feminine. It seems that men feel more connected to the term "Sacred Masculine," and women feel more connected to the term "Divine Feminine." Why is that? Is it simply a matter of terminology that has evolved differently amongst different groups?

I suggest that it's something deeper. I think the different terminology points to different things. And I think it's valuable for you to understand these differences as part of the bigger picture of understanding the differences between the Masculine and Feminine.

Let's begin with the term "Sacred Masculine." I see this term as similar to our expression of "the exalted Masculine." It's pointing to the higher path of the Masculine in reaching toward the divine. In this sense, it's connected to the idea of the Masculine being on a sacred quest. What the Masculine is seeking is the divine, in both its Masculine form of consciousness and its Feminine form of love.

You could see the Masculine as descending from pure consciousness into the world of incarnation and form or matter. The sacred journey of the Masculine is to maintain its connection to consciousness (or regain that connection if it's been lost in the process of incarnation) while simultaneously connecting with the Feminine form of the divine in matter. This journey of descent is another way of viewing the full descension process from pure Source into the third-dimensional realm.

The challenge for the Masculine is to maintain connection to the divine as consciousness while bringing that connection all the way down into life and ultimately honoring and loving the Feminine. This is what the Sacred Masculine does in its four aspects as sacred warrior, magician, lover, and king. It's a process of coming down into life as a divine journey, bringing the light of God into life.

The Feminine counterpart to the Sacred Masculine is the Divine Feminine. But the function of the Divine Feminine is different from the Sacred Masculine. As we've said before, the Divine Feminine is God in form or manifestation. Thus, the Divine Feminine is already descended, present as all form and matter.

The "work" for the Feminine is to recognize the Divine Feminine as themselves and "the all" and then to be that. It is not a journey in the way it is for the Sacred Masculine. It is rather an *opening in being* to the inherent divinity of all matter, all form—and an ability to be that divinity in its highest octave of love.

When the Feminine opens to its own divinity and the divinity in all, that one becomes extremely attractive as love. The Feminine thus attracts the Sacred Masculine, guiding the Masculine to the knowledge of the Divine Feminine that the Sacred Masculine seeks. The Feminine who has realized their own Divine Feminine nature opens to the Masculine in love and through that opening creates union with the Masculine.

From this place of union, the journey shifts. The quest of the third dimension of realizing love of the Feminine and union with the Feminine has been fulfilled. Now the next stage can begin, which you could see as a kind of U-turn into ascension. The ascension process is predicated on the fulfillment of the purpose of the descension process. The Sacred Masculine has descended to experience and love the Divine Feminine in form. Now they ascend in union.

This is the part of the process that humanity finds itself in now—and has actually been in for a very long time. In some ways you've "hit bottom" and are now turning around into the trajectory of ascension. The journey of ascension is a journey of return up through the dimensions, beginning with the next higher dimension, which for most of humanity is the fourth dimension.[31]

I hope this is clear. The Sacred Masculine is on a journey of descent, coming from pure consciousness (which is really the Divine Masculine) into the knowingness of the divine in form as the Divine Feminine. The Feminine is already descended, already present as the divine in all form. The "work" of the Feminine is to open to its own divinity (which is the Divine Feminine) in the already descended state of manifestation. When the Feminine opens to its own inherent divinity as Divine Feminine, it/he/she manifests the Divine Feminine quality of love. And this love attracts and guides the Masculine into union, from which both Masculine and Feminine may then begin the process of ascension. But this ascension is now in union, rather than the Masculine alone descending or the Feminine alone being already descended.

This is a summary of the spiritual journey for all humans. You are all descending from Source through your inner Masculine. For those manifesting outwardly in their Masculine aspect, this journey of descent is even more pronounced. This is why men in general (to the extent that they're manifesting from their Masculine) tend to be more "up" in their head and have more challenges with the earthier or "messier" parts of incarnate life, which generally refers to the Feminine aspects of life, such as emotions or living in the heart.

Similarly, you are all already descended because you are manifested in form. For those manifesting outwardly in their Feminine aspect, this quality of being already descended is even more pronounced. Women in general (to the extent that they're manifesting from their Feminine) tend to be more "down" in their bodies, sexuality, and emotions.[32]

Of course, these are generalizations, and each individual manifests their own unique mixture of Feminine and Masculine. Yet there is value in understanding these differences. This understanding engenders respect and valuing of the differences rather than discounting them. Such understanding also supports the full development of each individual's inner Masculine and Feminine. And ultimately, this understanding leads to love of these differences and union through the differences. As the expression in your world beautifully summarizes, "Viva la difference!"

EIGHTEEN

THE FEMININE IS CYCLIC

Mary Magdalene: I wish to continue our discussion of the Divine Feminine in your world.

In contrast to the Divine Masculine or consciousness (which exists outside of time), the Divine Feminine manifests in space and time. This is the same as saying that the Divine Feminine occurs in form or matter. And she manifests in a particular way in time. The Divine Feminine tends to occur in cycles.

You see these cycles in many ways, especially in nature. There is the daily cycle of the sun, which manifests as sunrise, midday, sunset, and night. There is a monthly cycle of the moon: new moon, waxing moon, full moon, waning moon, and dark of the moon. You have a yearly sun cycle that produces the seasons of spring, summer, fall, and winter, as well as the cycle of the spring equinox, summer solstice, autumn equinox, and winter solstice.

You also see cycles in humans. There is a monthly cycle of menstruation that women experience in their childbearing years. There is the cycle of human life from birth, to youth, to adult, to elder, and to death. For those of you who believe in reincarnation, there is the additional aspect of rebirth into another human lifetime and cycle. Even if you don't agree with the concept of reincarnation, rebirth can be seen as the beginning of new life in another, the carrying of the torch from one being to another, one generation to the next.

All of these cycles can be characterized as the larger cycle of birth, life, death, and rebirth. You see this cycle throughout nature and throughout all experience. Even human endeavors can be seen as beginning with a new idea or action, which is a form of birth. They continue through more ideas or actions, which is the life of that endeavor. And then they come to an end, which is death. Then there is rebirth in another form or endeavor.

The higher or sacred octave of the cycle of birth-life-death-rebirth can be described as creation, sustenance, and destruction. In your description of God, or various gods or goddesses, you often see these aspects portrayed as the "divine as creator" or "sustainer." It's less common to see the divine portrayed as destroyer, though you certainly have those figures in some of your spiritual traditions and stories.

Creation, sustenance, and destruction are truly the work of the Divine Feminine. Part of your spiritual work is to fully understand and honor all of these aspects of the Divine Feminine as manifestations of God, just as the Divine Masculine aspect of transcendence and consciousness is also to be understood and honored.

PART VI

UNION

NINETEEN

THE CIRCLE, THE CROSS, AND THE ARROW

Mary Magdalene: The symbol of the Divine Feminine is a circle. This represents the cyclic nature of the Feminine. The circle also symbolizes eternity because a circle has no beginning and no end. But it is a kind of eternity that happens in time and space.

The symbol of the Feminine in your contemporary time includes a cross coming down from the bottom of the circle. This cross represents humanity and human embodiment as your unique manifestation of the Divine Feminine.

The circle has another important meaning: it includes "the all." Specifically, the circle of the Feminine includes the Masculine. The Divine Feminine *always* includes the Masculine. This is different from the Masculine, which tends to exclude the Feminine in its focus on accomplishing goals. This is another reason why the Masculine needs the Feminine, because the Divine Feminine always includes both.

The symbol of the Masculine is an arrow pointed toward the sky. It is a symbol of goal orientation, of movement to accomplish a goal like an arrow shot from a bow, with the ultimate goal being the realization of transcendence and consciousness.

Yet the Masculine symbol also contains a circle as its base. The true meaning of this symbol is that the Masculine unites with the Feminine *as the base* for moving into higher realms of being and consciousness. Then they ascend together in their wholeness.

PART VII

THE CALL

TWENTY

THE PRAYER OF HEART-LIGHT

Received by Mercedes Kirkel

Sacred Masculine-Divine Feminine,
Great Oneness,
Light,
Love,
Here, now,
As all,
As me.

Provide what I need today
To live my purpose
For the highest good of all,
In love,
Forgiveness,
Peace,
Always with you.

From Mercedes: I received this prayer from my personal guides to help me stay connected to God as I healed from cancer treatment. The prayer is based on the Lord's Prayer from the Bible (Luke 11:2–4 and Matthew 6:9–13), but changed to carry the present teaching and blessing of Yeshua and Mary Magdalene.

In the Bible, Jesus used the Aramaic word "Abba" to address God when he prayed (Mark 14:36, and possibly in the original versions of the Lord's Prayer). "Abba" is an intimate, personal term for father. Similarly, "Imma" is the intimate, personal term for mother in Aramaic. I believe these terms reflect the loving, personal, and close relationship with God that Yeshua and Mary Magdalene had and still have.

For the opening line of this prayer, I sometimes say "Abba-Imma" instead of "Sacred Masculine-Divine Feminine." I do this because "Abba-Imma" powerfully connects me to Yeshua and Mary Magdalene, and because this more intimate way of addressing God particularly opens my heart.

I encourage you to find the names for God that most open your heart and create the strongest connection to the divine. If they are different from the names I offer here, I suggest you use your own words for the opening of the prayer.

Notes

1. "Yeshua" is the Aramaic name for Jesus. Many believe Jesus was called Yeshua when he was incarnated two thousand years ago, as Aramaic was the spoken language at that time in Israel. In Mercedes' channeled sessions, Mary Magdalene has always called Jesus "Yeshua." Accordingly, the name Yeshua is used in this book.

2. The Last Supper refers to the biblical account of the meal Jesus shared with his disciples before his crucifixion. It is described in Mark 14:12–26; Matthew 26:17–30; Luke 22:7–39; and John 13:1–17:26.

3. Joseph of Arimathea is referenced in the Bible as arranging the burial of Jesus after his crucifixion. See Mark 15:43–46; Matthew 27:57–60; Luke 23:50–54; and John 19:38–42.

4. Crucifixion was the form of capital punishment used by the Romans to execute Jesus. It involved nailing his body to a cross or beam, from which he hung until he was dead. Some believe Jesus survived the crucifixion.

5. The Templars were a Christian military order founded in France in 1119. They were formed to protect pilgrims on their journey to the Holy Land (Israel and Palestine). Templars later participated in the Crusades.

6. The term "Holy Land" refers to modern-day Israel and Palestine.

7. In 1312 (nearly two centuries after they were founded), the Templar Order was disbanded due to accusations of heresy and fraud. Templar leaders were tried, found guilty, and burned at the stake, which some consider the beginning of the Inquisition.

8. King Arthur was a legendary British leader, said to have ruled in the late fifth and early sixth centuries. Arthur created the Knights of the

Round Table, who were renowned for their heroic quests to fight injustice and for seeking the Holy Grail.

9. Mary Magdalene was a follower of Jesus in the Bible. Many believe she was Jesus's wife.

10. The term "sangreal" is another name for the Holy Grail. It's based on Old French, where *san* is translated as "holy" and *graal* or *greal* is translated as "cup." Others claim the term should be divided differently as "sang-real." This gives the term the meaning "royal blood," with *sang* translated as "royal" and *real* translated as "blood." Those asserting the latter interpretation say "sangreal" refers to the royal bloodline of Jesus and Mary Magdalene.

11. Twin flames are two souls who share the strongest kind of soul connection possible. Some believe that twin flames were originally one being that split into two souls, with one becoming Masculine and the other Feminine. Twin flames are profoundly connected, including sharing the same soul purpose.

12. The term "Christ" comes from the Greek word *Christos*, meaning "anointed." In his communications to Mercedes, Yeshua stated that "Christ" means "anointed one." In biblical times, ceremonial anointing was a symbol that God had chosen and set apart that person for a particular role.

13. Similar to the term "Christ" (see note 12), "Messiah" comes from the Hebrew word *mashiach*, which means "anointed one."

14. In the Old Testament, the term "son of God" is used to refer to humans who have a special relationship with God. In the New Testament, the term is applied to Jesus.

15. The terms "Divine Feminine" or "Divine Masculine" refer to the Feminine or Masculine aspects of God or our human divinity.

16. The terms "Feminine" and "Masculine" refer to the archetypal Feminine and Masculine that reside within all of us (regardless of our gender) and within all of manifestation. The twin concepts are similar to the concepts of yin and yang in Eastern philosophy.

The Feminine aspects of our humanness relate to our body, energy, emotions, sexuality, and heart. The highest form of the Feminine is pure love. The Masculine aspects of our humanity relate to the mind and will-power. The highest form of the Masculine is pure consciousness.

An in-depth explanation of the Masculine and the Feminine can be found in *Mary Magdalene Beckons* by Mercedes Kirkel, www.mercedeskirkel.com.

17. An individual's soul path involves the course of their soul during their total incarnations. One's soul path is based on agreements the individual makes prior to each incarnation ("soul agreements") and the choices they make in that lifetime through free will.

18. "The Accolade" (1901) by Edmund Leighton.

19. "All You Need Is Love" is the title and one of the lyrics of a song by the English rock band the Beatles. The song was released in 1967.

20. In Hinduism, *Kundalini* is a form of Divine Feminine energy located at the base of the spine. When activated, Kundalini is believed to lead to spiritual awakening.

21. The Garden of Eden is part of the story of creation in the Old Testament of the Bible. In the story, Adam and Eve (the first man and woman) live in a paradisiacal garden in innocent nakedness and bliss. They're free to eat from any tree in the garden except the "tree of knowledge of good and evil." Tempted by a serpent, Eve eats the forbidden fruit and shares it with Adam. As a result, Adam and Eve's "eyes are opened" and they become ashamed of their nakedness, covering themselves with fig leaves. God declares punishments for their transgression and expels them from the garden, thus losing their access to the "tree of life," which gives immortality.

22. Consciousness is the quality or state of being aware.

23. "Container of love" doesn't mean to contain or limit the Feminine. Rather, it is a sphere or circle of love around the Feminine, created by the Masculine to protect, honor, and support her.

24. In Hinduism, the Feminine quality of energy or radiance is known as *Shakti*.

25. This talk was given on the Feast Day of Mary Magdalene. Mary is referencing the people who are celebrating her on this day.

26. Mary is referring to Mercedes's books, courses, retreats, and private sessions.

27. Descension is the process by which God has manifested in form in progressively lower dimensions of reality, ending in the third dimension. Ascension is the process that leads third-dimensional beings back into progressively higher dimensions of reality.

28. See note 27.

29. Mary is referring to John 14:12 in the Bible.

30. The higher self is the part of one's being that is in union with the divine.

31. In the book *Mary Magdalene Beckons*, Mary Magdalene presents a model of our universe that includes twelve dimensions. The fourth dimension is the next plane of reality beyond the third dimension. This plane is energetically rather than physically based. The full model of the twelve dimensions, including the fourth dimension, is described in detail in *Mary Magdalene Beckons* by Mercedes Kirkel, www.mercedeskirkel.com.

32. Because sexuality is based in both the physical and energetic aspects of our being, it is a Feminine part of manifestation. An individual's experience of sexual energy, as well as their physical sexual responses, are part of their inner Feminine.

About the Author

MERCEDES KIRKEL is a multi-award-winning, bestselling author and channel for Yeshua and Mary Magdalene.

In the summer of 2010, Mary Magdalene began coming to Mercedes daily, giving extraordinary messages for humanity's evolution and spiritual growth. That was the birth of the first book in the Magdalene-Yeshua Teachings, *Mary Magdalene Beckons: Join the River of Love*.

Since then, Mary Magdalene and Yeshua have continued to communicate through Mercedes, delivering illuminating messages about the sacred partnership of the Divine Feminine and Masculine and guiding people in their spiritual development.

Based in New Mexico, Mercedes offers online and in-person courses and events. Her specialties include spiritual direction and heart coaching.

> Learn more about Mercedes and her work at:
> www.mercedeskirkel.com.

Books and Videos by Mercedes Kirkel

THE MAGDALENE-YESHUA TEACHING BOOKS

Mary Magdalene Beckons: Join the River of Love
The Holy Grail: Sacred Masculine & Divine Feminine
Dialogues with Yeshua and Mary Magdalene: The Journey to Love
The Heart Path of Mary Magdalene: A Guide to Living from Your Heart
Sublime Union: A Woman's Sexual Odyssey Guided by Mary Magdalene

THE HEART PATH VIDEO COURSE

A video course of Mercedes coaching people in the Heart Path, using exercises and real-life demonstrations.

All available at: www.mercedeskirkel.com

www.ingramcontent.com/pod-product-compliance
Ingram Content Group UK Ltd.
Pitfield, Milton Keynes, MK11 3LW, UK
UKHW020649250325
5143UKWH00034B/502